Teaching English as a Second Language

Teaching English as a Second Language

A Guide for Teaching Children

(TESL or TEFL)

By: David Chapman

Order this book online at www.trafford.com
or email orders@trafford.com

Most Trafford titles are also available at major online book retailers.

Printed in the United States of America.

ISBN: 978-1-4269-5257-9 (sc)
ISBN: 978-1-4269-5258-6 (e)

Trafford rev.01/13/2011

 www.trafford.com

North America & International
toll-free: 1 888 232 4444 (USA & Canada)
phone: 250 383 6864 ♦ fax: 812 355 4082

TABLE OF CONTENTS

Acknowledgements

There are several people I would like to take some time to thank. Without these people in my life, there is no way this book could've been created.

First and far most, without question the first people I have to thank were all of my students, and there were hundreds of them. They were the ones who challenged me to become a better teacher every day. There was never a dull moment, helping all these children learn English was a very rewarding experience indeed. It is the real reason I wrote this book, it was to make sure that class was always fun and productive for them. I wish them all great success and a happy future, I miss you all!

Second, I would like to thank my older sister who has always encouraged me to write. Without her constant encouragement and financial support this book may never have been published.

Thirdly, I must thank my younger sister who is also a teacher and reviewed my book and shared her opinions and gave input during the early stages of writing.

I would also like to thank my Mom and Dad who taught me to love and care for people. It is because of them that I realize how important it is to help others.

I cannot forget my brother. Thank you for doing so many favors for me, even if it was just buying me a coffee at Tim Horton's or the time you offered me a place to stay at your home when I first came back from Asia. You are an amazingly kind individual and I wish you nothing but the best.

Also, special thanks to all the parents who spent a lot of money to have their kids / my students learn English. I would never of had the opportunity to go overseas and enrich my life the way I did if it weren't for you. Thank you!

Thank you Taiwan! This is where I spent most of my time teaching English as a second language. What a wonderful country you have and what wonderful people you are. I had the time of my life and I can't wait to go back and visit or teach again soon.

Thank you.

Introduction

About this Teaching Guide

1. The following TESL / TEFL guide (Teaching English as a Second Language or Teaching English as a Foreign Language) is what I have come up with so far in my exciting career of almost 10 years as an ESL Teacher. It is a summary of all my teaching ideas, combined with the games & activities that I use for teaching English as a second language to children. The purpose of this guide is to show you what you can teach children, what you can do with your students and how to teach them. But, don't stop here. Go out and find better strategies for teaching. Go out and find more games & activities that work for you. Do whatever you need to do to become a better teacher and I would strongly encourage you to do those things. This is a guide that I made and I strongly feel will give a new teacher that much needed helping hand or an experienced teacher a few fresh reminders and some new ideas. I wish someone gave me this guide when I first started teaching English as a second language, that's for sure!

2. Obviously your school should have a curriculum for you and they should have materials and books that you can use to teach with. But, the reality is unfortunately many schools have very short and poor curriculums. Even in the best schools you will still find yourself with a lot of lesson planning and time to do your own things in class. This is just part of being a teacher. I hope this guide can

help fill in some of that 'dead' time and I hope this guide can give you lots of ideas on how to run your class.

3. I know this isn't a complete guide to everything you need to know, but I did my best to simplify and organize it to only include information that works, and will be useful for you. Nothing in this guide is filler, just there to fill space. Every game, every activity, every point is the best ideas I have come across. All the things that didn't work for me have been discarded, they are not included in this guide. I have used all the games and activities in this guide over and over again in my own classrooms. And often, have used the same game or activity with just one class over 100 times. I also hope this guide will get your mind thinking about the right ideas on how to teach your class and how to make your class more fun and successful. Good luck!

<u>Get Ready for Some Hard Work</u>

1. Never forget that teaching is an ongoing and never ending process to always be on the ball. You need to expend a lot of energy every day. You need to always try your best if you truly want to be an effective teacher.

2. The most important thing you can do is work hard and give your best effort. The more effort you put into your work, the more you will get out of it. The more effort you put into your teaching, the better teacher you can be. The better teacher you can be, the more your students can benefit from you. The more your students benefit from you, the more your students will learn. The more your students learn, the more you will learn about how other people learn. You are not only teaching the students, you are teaching yourself about intelligence. It's a win / win situation.

3. Have fun with it! The more fun and entertainment you can create in your classroom, the more fun your students

will have. The more fun your students have, the more fun you will have. Another win / win situation.

Becoming a Teacher is a Huge Responsibility

1. You chose to be a teacher. If you wanted to, you could of chose to do anything you wanted, but you chose to be a teacher.

2. Becoming a teacher is taking on an enormous responsibility. If you wanted a laid back, chilled out job, you chose the wrong job!

3. You are now the guide for each child's future. You will have everlasting effects on each student you come across. What you say might be remembered by a child forever. What you do and how you act, your students will follow your lead. How much you teach them, and how well they learn will stick with them forever. They can't change this, they can't go back and do it again. They are only a child once, so give them the best chance possible to be smart and succeed.

4. When you decide to work with children, their lives, their futures are in your hands. You can't be lazy, they are our future! If you want to be a lazy and chilled out employee, please choose another job.

5. Thank you for choosing to work hard. The children, their parents, the school, their country, our whole world and the future appreciate it. Thanks a lot!

Structure In The Classroom

Keeping Your Classroom Under Control

1. Children need guidance. Just letting your students do anything they want creates chaos and is an incorrect learning environment for the children to experience.
2. Being firm, enforcing rules and showing professionalism around your students will have a positive effect on the whole class.
3. Keeping your classroom under control ensures safety for all. If you allow your classroom to run away from you and you lose control of it. Your students could become in dangerous situations and they will not be learning correctly. A very sad situation indeed.
4. If your class is not under control, things slide, chaos erupts, and the children lose all their respect and learning potential. It becomes a nightmare for the kids and the teacher.

When Your Classroom Is Under Control

1. When you are firm (or strict) and set rules, it is easier to accomplish more things during class, including playing games. You can do things at a faster and smoother pace. Therefore, the class ends up being more fun.
2. Your students will pay better attention in class and can easily absorb the knowledge that is being taught to them.
3. Your students will learn faster. Class will be more interesting for them because they will be paying more

attention to things going on in the class. If class is more interesting, then learning becomes more fun.

4. Your students will develop good work habits and be learning properly.

5. If you try to be the nicest teacher in the world and don't enforce any rules, your class will end up out of control. Doing activities in class, including games and teaching lectures become slower processes and are harder and more frustrating to do. Not only for you, but for most of your students too. Therefore, learning ends up not being fun. Your class will lose their motivation to learn English properly.

Continue To Aim For A Fun Class

1. You still need to be positive and make the class as fun as possible. Just because you have set firm rules for your classroom doesn't mean your class needs to be boring. Your class can be the most exciting and entertaining class around if you want it to be. Being firm just means you expect your students to follow certain guidelines, and to respect their authority and each other. They must learn to respect your role as a teacher and in turn you must respect who they are.

Giving Out Consequences (Punishments)

1. Keep reminding your students all the time why they need to be good and explain to them how to be good. What are the classroom rules? Put them on the wall & review them. Tell them over and over again and don't ever stop telling them.

2. It is very important to have a set of rules & guidelines for you students to follow. It is a great way to provide structure for your class. Consequences are needed as children will always try to push the limits. Now, your students will know what is expected of them and if

they choose to break a rule, they are choosing to take a consequence.

3. Stay calm & relaxed when giving out a consequence. You should always feel in control of the situation. Take a deep breath, slow down and have patience.

4. Make sure when you say you will do something, you always do that something. Don't make exceptions for a child or lighten up on the consequence you originally stated. Be consistent so that when you give out a consequence, it is a done deal, there is no turning back. This way your students will always take your verbal reminders seriously. You will often just have to give out a warning or a stern look in order to keep your class in control.

Examples of Consequences (Punishments)

1. Take away one minute of their playtime or break-time. One minute for each infraction that could add up to 5, 10, 12, or 18 minutes. It could be for the whole playtime, so no playtime for that child today. They must sit at their desk or sit somewhere else while all the well behaved students play. You can keep track of every minute you give by printing the student's name in the corner on your whiteboard and keep marking a line beside their name as they misbehave.

2. The misbehaved student can't play in the next game in class. Example: A sticky ball game or whiteboard game. Have them sit off to the side so they can still see and hear and learn, they just can't participate.

3. Give that one student the 'very disappointed look' with your eyes. Look them straight in the eyes and show them how disappointed you are with their poor behavior.

4. Have them stand in the corner or sit in a chair far away from the group.

5. Have the child who is misbehaving sit at a different table than the others.

6. Have the whole class go to their table and put their heads down for a 1, 2, 3, 4 or 5 minute time out. Nobody can say a word or the whole class must start over again.

7. For continuing problems, bring the student to the office with the manager and sit them down for a stern and serious talk. Explain to them what is happening and why. Talk about the consequences that may happen if this behavior continues. Also, talk about rewards and all the good things that will happen to the child if they change their behavior and start being good. This should shake the child up and show them that you are serious about them changing.

Examples of Encouraging (Rewards)

1. Use positive reinforcements the most, as much as possible, almost always.

2. Be consistent and be fair with every single student in the class. Don't just pick on one student or spoil another.

3. For younger children, make sure you always have a positive reinforcement board somewhere in the classroom. Print every one of your student's names down the left side on the whiteboard. As the day goes on, you draw little happy faces or stars beside their name when they do something good. If they misbehave you can erase their happy face or star or can even give them an X. Then, at the end of the day turn their happy faces into tangible rewards. (Example: tokens)

4. Try to give most of your rewards for effort, students who are trying their hardest. Not always just for students who made the best story or who got the highest mark on the test. Who is trying the hardest should get the most rewards.

5. Verbally encourage your students continuously. Don't discourage them by complaining and acting all frustrated when they get something wrong or make a mistake over

and over again. Encourage them and help them achieve their goals. Never give up!

6. When they are good, tell them. Don't say nothing, but tell them over and over again how good they are. They will love to hear it and continue to be good because of it.

7. Smile at a child and verbally praise them when they do something good. Go out of your way to do this and do this as often as possible.

8. Laugh with your students, bond with them, get to know them. They will get to know you and respect you for being such a genuine person.

9. Take time to speak with each child individually. Listen to their stories, ask them questions, help them, and quite simply just show them that you care.

10. Give out lots of reward cards or school points. Many schools already have their own reward system in place. Use it.

11. Give out some light candy, a chocolate or a drink.

12. Hand out stickers or small toys for a reward.

13. Have a class party for the whole class if everyone is good for a pre-determined time period. (Example: If everyone only uses English in class for a 1 month period and they don't use their native language, then throw a 30 minute 'English" party for them. Go to the store, buy some drinks and buy some food and play some music and have a party, the students will love it! (and you will love that they are only speaking English everyday)

14. Use anything and everything you have for prizes and rewards.

Example of Classroom Rules

1. Always sit properly.
2. Raise your hand to speak.
3. Listen to people when they are talking.
4. Make good lines when we line up.
5. Don't be crazy & silly all day long.
6. Be nice to everyone and share with your friends.
7. ONLY SPEAK ENGLISH!!!

The Four Corners
of Teaching English

Reading

1. Read, read, and read some more of anything and everything you can possibly find. Let your students practice reading everything you come across. Read any page you can from their text books & workbooks. Read the instructions in their books together as a class. Print and photocopy reading material for them from online. Bring in a new story book and have everyone read it once. Print a few sentences on the whiteboard and read it as a class etc.

2. Review phonics and all the blended phonics sounds as often as possible. Or at least until they have it down without any problems.

3. When the class is reading, make everyone sound good or stop them. In general, the teacher should not read while the class is reading. You should be listening for their mistakes and stop them to correct it, or wait until they finish reading and correct their mistakes afterwards.

4. You can have them read together as a whole class.

5. You can have them read in different groups.

6. You can have them read quietly to themselves.

7. You can have them listen to you read.

8. You can have a discussion after your read.

9. You can ask oral questions to individual students after you read.

10. You can write questions on the whiteboard related to the reading and have them copy the questions out and then answer them in their notebook. The answers need to be in full sentences, not one or two word answers.

Writing

1. Writing is a very difficult skill to master and therefore takes a lot of practice. Your students will often moan and groan anytime you give them a writing assignment. It is challenging for them, it is work for them. Therefore, whenever possible guide them and help them write. Don't just say "Ok everyone. Write a story". How do you write a story? Show them how to do what you want them to do. Give them examples, give them a pattern to follow, give them a template. Make sure you give them something to guide them on what to write.

2. When you have your students write something, have them bring it up to you when they are finished and correct it with a red pen in front of their eyes. Now, they'll see where they made their mistakes right away. Always have them write it again the correct way. Many teachers will just collect all the work, take it home, mark it in red pen and hand it out to the students the next class. The students will not look to see exactly where they made their mistakes. So, as often as possible make sure you show them their writing mistakes right in front of their eyes during class.

Listening

1. The best way to improve your students listening skills is to have an English only classroom & also to make sure your students pay attention during class. Don't let your class get out of control and all your students will be listening. It is that simple.

2. Your students do so much listening in your class that you don't need to work on this area as much. It just happens naturally. Try to concentrate your efforts on the other three areas of English the most; writing, speaking, and reading.

<u>Speaking</u>

1. Correct their pronunciation. If you hear one student who makes an incorrect pronunciation of a word, stop! Stop whatever you are doing and print that word on the whiteboard and teach the whole class how to pronounce it properly. Chances are some of the other students mispronounce it too. Now, everyone can see how this word is pronounced correctly. (Example: <u>ski</u> <u>ing</u> or <u>con</u> <u>tin</u> <u>ue)</u> It is an ongoing battle that will never go away. Keep working at it and be very strict with your students on their pronunciation.

2. Don't have the class repeat the newly learned vocabulary just once. Repeat the newly learned vocabulary two times, three times, four times, five times.

3. Make sure all the students speak loud and clearly just like you. Don't let them get away with mumbling and whispering their answers. Have them speak with confidence.

4. Make sure all the students speak in full grammatically correct sentence forms. It may sound a bit silly to be speaking English in full sentences all the time, but these students are learning English as a second language. They need to practice how to speak it correctly before they go off using short-forms and slang. Ask questions and always expect answers in full grammatically correct sentence forms. It is a very important routine to get into.

What Else To Teach

Phonics (Pronunciation)

(An outline of what phonics to teach & review, review, review)

Upper Case Letters and Sound Recognition
A B C D E F G H I J K L M N O P Q R S T U V W X Y Z

Lower Case Letters
a b c d e f g h i j k l m n o p q r s t u v w x y z

Short Vowel Sounds
A E I O U and sometimes Y

Long Vowel Sounds
Long A = (a_e) (ai) (ay)
Long E = (e_e) (ea) (ee)
Long I = (i_e) (ie) (igh)
Long O = (o_e) (ow) (oa)
Long U = (u_e) (ue) (oo)
Long Y = The long E sound is when the word has another vowel in it like baby
Long Y = The long I sound is when the word has no other vowel in it like cry

Beginning Sounds
(bl) (cl) (fl) (gl) (pl) (sl)

(dr) (br) (cr) (fr) (gr) (pr) (tr) (wr)

(sn) (sm) (st) (sc) (sp) (sk) (sw)

(th) (sh) (ch) (ph) (wh) (kn)

Ending Sounds
(ing)

(s) (es)

(mp) (ck) (rd) (nd) (ts) (lk) (tle) (nt) (ch) (th)

(er) (ir) (ur)

New Vocabulary

1. You should always be feeding your students with as much new vocabulary as you can. You can get new vocabulary from anywhere and everywhere. Just look in their books, talk with them, keep doing new lessons, a new word will always come up. Stop, explain it, talk about it, have them make a sentence with it and move on.

2. Keep track of all the new words your class comes across by writing them down in a separate file. Now, you can easily pull out that file and review, review, review, or use those words to play a game, do an activity, or do an assignment.

Verbs

1. Teach your students every verb you can think of. Have them change the verb into its different tenses by changing a target sentence to reflect each tense. Example: I swim. (I swam, I am swimming, I will swim) They can do it verbally for you, or have them write it out in their workbooks.

2. Write down and have a list of verbs in a separate file. Now, you can easily pull out that file and review, review, review, or use those verbs to play a game, do an activity, or do an assignment.

<u>The Six Main Verb Tenses</u>
Past Continuous...........................I was walking down the street.
Past Simple...I walked down the street.
Present Simple.......................................I walk the street.
Present continuous.......................I am walking down the street.
Future simple ....I will walk down the street.
Future continuous..................I will be walking down the street.

<u>Grammar</u>

1. Remember when teaching new grammar points to keep it simple. Take it slow, give lots of examples and give your students lots of time to practice. It may seem like common sense to you, but this is brand new stuff for them.
2. Your students don't necessarily need to know the terminology and complexities of what you are teaching them. They often just need to know the basis of it and be able to apply it to their English work.
3. Keep track of all the newly learned grammar points you teach to your students. Write down these grammar points in a file. Now, you can easily pull out that file and review, review, review, or use those grammar points to play a game, do an activity, or do an assignment.

<u>Homework</u>

1. Always assign homework for older classes. Keep it straightforward with nothing overly challenging. Just something that will get their brain thinking in English or reviewing a newly taught concept at home. Keep the challenging stuff for in the classroom when you can be

there to help them. There is no need to frustrate your students, keep their confidence up.

2. Always use a red pen to mark & correct with. Do not use other colors, red is easily seen and is the common color a teacher corrects with. It looks professional.

Examples of Homework
1. Write out 5 questions on the whiteboard. They must copy the question and answer each one in full sentence structure at home in their workbooks.
2. Write their weekly spelling words 3 times each.
3. Write a personal journal for homework every two weeks. Give them a journal book for this.
4. Have them write a short story. They can read it or you can read their stories at the beginning of next class.
5. Take 10 of the newly learned vocabulary words and have them write a short story using these words in their story.
6. Have students draw a picture for homework. Then, at the beginning of the next class each student must come to the front of the room and describe what they have drawn.
7. Watch an English T.V. show for homework. Have them come to the next class and discuss with everyone what they watched for homework.
8. Do their workbook. Example: Pages 24-26 for homework.
9. Read their textbook. Example: Pages 38-45 for homework.

Review, Review, Review (The 3 R's of Teaching)
1. Reviewing is one of the most important things you can do with your students. I can't emphasize this point enough. This is the golden rule, the three R's of teaching. You can never get enough of it.

2. Teach, teach and teach your students all sorts of new things. But, never forget to go back to previously taught lessons and review.
3. Some things won't need any reviewing, some things may need to be reviewed just two or three times, and some things may need to be reviewed all year long.
4. When you run out of things to do, review, review, review. (play a game or do an activity) Now, you'll always have something to do.

Only Speak English!!!

1. This is by far the most important rule to have established in your classroom and hopefully your whole school. This is also such an easy rule to follow once everyone in your class or at your school gets used to it. It becomes the norm.
2. Your students have all the time in the world to speak their native language at home and in their own lives outside of English school. But, I have heard teachers tell me that the students are unable to speak English all the time, because it is too difficult, we would be asking them to do something too hard for them. I believe this to be 100% incorrect. There is a reason it is too difficult for everyone to communicate in English all the time. When the students and the teaching staff are speaking their native language half the time, getting into an English mindset does become impossible. Practice in an 'English only' environment and the students in your class will pick up English faster than you could ever imagine. They will become little sponges and absorb far more of the English language than if you let them stay in their native language half of the time.

My Teaching Philosophy

1. I have read about it and believe that the best way for people to learn a second language is when they are using it to communicate with the world around them. When they are using it to get their point across, for their own purpose, for their own interest. To complete a task, to talk to their friends, to win a competition etc. Children do not learn English as a second language as well when it is being taught in the form of a lecture for studious learning. This is just too boring and un-interesting for them. They barely retain any of the new language being taught.

2. You can't just teach English from a book like a professor by lecturing and giving out an absurd amount of information and knowledge day after day. You have to involve your students in activities, competitions, have them get up and use the language for themselves. They have to practice it, they have to use it. It will stick in their minds much more clearly, much easier, much faster, and with much more enjoyment.

3. Don't get me wrong, you will sometimes have to lecture, you will have to teach, and your students will have to sit down and consciously learn what is being taught to them. But, as much and as often as possible create an environment where your students have to and hopefully want to use English to communicate with the people around them. In the form of writing, listening, speaking, and reading.

More Tips

Teaching Tips

1. <u>Keep eye contact with your students as much as possible</u>. Look around the room and look into their eyes, let them know you are there. Don't just stare at the back of the room or at one or two students. Example: That smart kid who is always participating, that misbehaving attention seeker, try to look at everyone.

2. <u>Don't let the children talk amongst each other while you are talking</u>. When the teacher is talking, students listen. When anyone is talking at the front of the class whether it is you, a guest speaker or another student, everyone listens. This is called respect and can easily be followed if you enforce it as a classroom rule.

3. <u>Speak loud and clear</u>. Enunciate your words. Your students need to hear your voice in order for things to stick. Don't get me wrong, there is no need for shouting in class, but speaking loudly and clearly is very important. It ensures that everything you say is heard and understood by everyone. Although, sometimes using different voice levels can be very effective too. If you talk very quietly, the students must really listen to hear what you are saying.

4. <u>Speak slower than normal and only use vocabulary that your students will understand</u>. Don't just go into class and speak in the same complex ways as you would to other native English speakers. Don't speak so fast and naturally that everything you say is going over their heads. Slow your pace down, figure out what level your students are

at and speak in the simplest sentence structure that suits their English level. Still use the correct grammar, but keep it to simple vocabulary. As your students advance, you can start speaking at a more regular pace and using more advanced vocabulary.

5. Teach at an even pace, but a fairly quick pace. Keep teaching at a consistent and steady pace. Focus on the main point, and move on.

6. When a disruption occurs, it is ok, it happens. Just stop it quickly and immediately get back to what you were doing. Example: A mosquito enters the classroom, another teacher enters the room, or a kid falls off their chair. These things happen, there is no need to make a big deal of it, just don't let it evolve into a bigger issue, deal with it and move on ASAP.

7. Move around the room. Don't always stand in one spot. Moving makes you look more lively and energetic.

8. Wait for your students to be quiet by looking out at the class with eerie silence. Keep waiting, and keep staring out until they all get your drift.

9. Make sure your students have nothing on their desks when you are lecturing a class. Not a pencil case, not a pen, not even a book. They need to listen to you and if they have anything at all on their desk it will easily distract them.

10. Start simple and then build up. Example: Don't start at a full sentence. Teach them the vocabulary first, teach them today's grammar point second, then work on the whole sentence or paragraph last.

11. Keep it Simple Stupid. (KISS) Don't try so hard that you end up explaining things in an overly sophisticated manner. Keep things simple and straightforward and let your students do a lot of their learning by simply trying to do it themselves. Hands on learning, not just a bunch of lecturing and hours of explanations. Let your students

do it, figure out where their mistakes are, and go from there.

Classroom Tips

1. <u>Make letters and pictures on the whiteboard as big as you can</u>. Bigger the better. There is never a time when you print too big on the whiteboard. The bigger it is, the easier it will be for the kids to see and absorb the information you are trying to give them.
2. <u>Class becomes very boring if the teacher is doing all the talking</u>. Talk as little as you possibly can, keep your lectures short and to the point. Have the students talk as often as possible. Class will be more entertaining for them.
3. <u>Expand on anything interesting and be as bizarre as they want</u>. Give tons of examples, ask them questions, make jokes, follow their conversations, act things out, tell stories etc.
4. <u>Focus on all four areas of English, not just one</u>. Example: Don't just always work on speaking and listening activities. Make sure you do lots of activities on reading & writing too.
5. <u>Learn everyone's name ASAP</u>. Not just in your class, but the whole school if you can. And use their names as often as possible. Everyone likes to hear their name called.

Make a Lesson Plan for Every Class

1. <u>Come to class prepared and keep your class as structured as possible</u>. Organize yourself and plan your lessons ahead of time. Write down everything you want to accomplish in class today. What game and activity are you going to use? What pages in their books do you have to cover. What new concept are you going to teach today? How are you going to teach it? Do you need to bring any props to class? Write out a short and simple lesson plan

and bring it to every class. Don't start to figure out what you are going to do and what pages need to be covered during the actual class time. Plan ahead and always bring that plan on paper to class with you. Your classes will run much more smoothly.

2. <u>When you are prepared, it will put your students in a routine.</u> Routines help eliminate unwanted bad behavior by the children.

<u>Have Fun!</u>

1. <u>Create competition amongst the students often.</u> This will cause the class to immediately pay attention, they will learn better and things will stick because it is interesting and exciting. They will always want to pay attention and participate because they want to win!

2. <u>As much as possible, get the children into groups and speaking amongst each other.</u> This is way more fun than having to talk to the teacher all the time.

3. <u>Bad acting is always good, so do it.</u> Your students will laugh at you no matter if it was good acting or bad acting. Therefore, act out things whenever possible.

4. <u>Choose all the students, not just the few outgoing ones.</u> I find it is the middle ability students who are left out the most, as teachers are always constantly focusing on the smartest and problem kids. Don't do this, involve the whole class.

5. <u>Be fair to all students at all times.</u> Don't let certain children get away with more or less than another child. Make sure everyone is following the same rules.

6. <u>Never get angry, be in control at all times and always strive for fun.</u>

7. <u>Have lots of prizes and keep consistent with your discipline.</u> Rewards and consequences are so important. This is how you can easily manage to control your class without yelling.

Be a Positive Role Model

1. <u>Be enthusiastic and up the pace, the children will follow your lead</u>. You need to have energy.

2. <u>You need a positive attitude, and you need to show that attitude to your students all the time</u>. Always enter your class with this positive attitude.

3. <u>Praise and encourage your students as much as possible</u>. All children feel great about themselves when they are recognized. Recognize when they make a good effort and most importantly tell them about it.

4. <u>Your kids will mimic your attitude</u>. If you are lazy, your kids will become lazy too. If you have an "I don't care" attitude, your students won't care either. If you have energy and enthusiasm, your kids will have more energy and enthusiasm too.

5. <u>Give out rewards for good behavior and for successful accomplishments</u>. Many schools will have reward cards or a point structure or something of this sort. You should also give out your own rewards. Example: stickers, candy, verbal praise, give a kid a high five, make a successful student the winner and they can come with the teacher to get stuff from the office etc. Be sure to be consistent and fair to everyone.

6. <u>Be friendly to your co-teacher, if you have one</u>. You will be working alongside each other all year long. Understand your differences, different cultures, different ways of teaching children, differences between a male approach to working with children and a woman approach to working with children. Western culture vs. their Culture. There are a lot of differences that you'll need to work through.

Be Firm & Have Some Expectations
for your Class to Follow

1. <u>Have consequences (punishments) ready for bad behavior and don't hesitate to use them.</u> Use this form of negative reinforcement as rarely as possible. But, when a student deserves a consequence, you need to give it to them, be consistent with this. It will let your students know where you draw the line. It will let them know that you won't take disrespect and bad behavior from them, and that you are serious. If you fail to follow through on your consequences when a child is misbehaving, other children will notice this and your class will begin to push and push you to test your limits. Don't let your class push you over, set your limits early on. It will keep things a lot easier for you in the long-term.

2. <u>Definitely don't have a mean attitude, but you must be firm and serious with your students.</u> You are their teacher, not their friend. Your job is to guide them into learning, not to show them you are the friendliest person on the planet. Don't get me wrong, like them, help them, get to know them, be as friendly as you can with them, become buddies with them, whatever. But, never forget that you are their teacher, not their friend! There is a big difference.

3. <u>Avoid abusing your voice.</u> Raise your voice and yell as little as you possibly can. Then, when you do raise your voice and yell, the children will immediately get your drift and pay attention. If you are raising your voice and yelling all the time, you become background noise for the students, and they won't take you serious anymore when you yell.

Teaching Younger Students (Under 10 years old)

1. <u>Physical activities are excellent and you should use them as much as possible to get the kids up and doing things.</u>

2. <u>The younger they are, the more they need to move around the room.</u> With the youngest of students have them standing every 10 to 15 minutes. Example: Go over there, make two lines, make a circle, do this, do that, play a game etc. Then, go sit down again, but only for 10 to 15 minutes. Obviously, the older the children, the longer they can sit.

3. <u>Sometimes your students may just need a few moments to go crazy.</u> Let them go crazy. Tell them they have 1 minute to go crazy, then they have to come sit down properly and get ready for class as a mature student. They might need to release stress, they have lots of youthful energy, they enjoy being immature, they are being kids.

4. <u>Have younger kids do things for you.</u> Example: Erase the whiteboard, get you markers, pass out the work books etc. Many children like to do that stuff.

5. <u>To get the attention of very young kids at the beginning of class, give them commands.</u> Such as touch your nose, touch your eyes, stand up, turn around, sit down etc. This gives them something to do, something to start focusing their attention to you.

Keep Learning / Keep Finding New Ideas / Keep Becoming a Better Teacher

1. <u>Always keep your eyes and ears open to learn new games and activities to bring to your class.</u> Also learn new strategies and styles for teaching. Improve your method.

2. <u>You can find many helpful sites online to help you with your teaching.</u> There are sites for games & activities, sites to give you visual aids or sounds for your teaching, sites for improving your method of teaching etc. Go online and search for some good websites and then keep track of what sites you found. Write them down, so you don't forget them.

Teaching Ideas

Older Classes (Over 10 years old)

1. <u>Review and teach all phonics possible</u>. (keep your own phonics file)
2. <u>Review and teach all verbs</u>. (keep your own verb file)
3. <u>Review and teach all grammar points you can come up with</u>. (keep your own grammar file) Constantly be correcting their grammar and pronunciation mistakes.
4. <u>Review all kinds of target sentence patterns</u>. (keep a list of target sentence patterns on file)
5. <u>Review the tenses</u>. Don't forget to apply simple and continuous to your tenses. (Past continuous, past simple, present continuous, present simple, future continuous, future simple) Everyone in the class should know these tenses and be able to apply them to practical English work.
6. <u>Read something, anything</u>. Do a lot of work on reading stuff and understanding what they just read.
7. <u>Have a spelling test</u>. Then, have the students correct each other's work while you go over and print the answers on the whiteboard.
8. <u>Check and correct their school workbooks immediately after they do it</u>. Have them bring it up to you, or put their hand up and go to their desk. Make sure everything in their workbook is marked in red pen. If a page is not completed by a student because they were absent or something, have them do it now. All bookwork should

be completely marked and up to date. Their parents will be happy to see this.

9. <u>Keep track of their marks on a bulletin board.</u> <u>Give them marks for effort, test scores, reading ability etc.</u> Everyone can see where they stand. It's another form of competition for them. To see yourself at the top gives you pride and confidence. To see yourself at the bottom is embarrassing and may encourage that student to try harder.

10. <u>Check their homework at the beginning of every single class.</u> If they completed their homework, that is great and verbally reward them. If their homework is not complete, that is ok. Make them still do it for the next class, but add some extra form of homework because they forgot. Now they will have three pieces of homework. The homework they forgot, the extra homework you just gave them, and today's homework. If they continue to forget, keep adding more homework for them, and make sure they complete it! Eventually, everyone in class will be doing their homework because no student wants extra work to do.

11. <u>Keep on your students about only speaking English in class.</u> Make a small poster and put everyone's name on it. Have a 10 X's system where if they get 10 X's then there is no party for them at the end of the month. If they don't get 10 X's, they can join the party. They have a chance to say their native language only ten times in your class during the month or then they must miss out on the English party. Be strict with this rule. Any of their native language at all and bang! They get an X right away, no questions asked. This is consistency and fairness for everyone. This is my favorite way to keep my classroom speaking in only English. It is easy, I never need to get angry, I just smile and say "X". They may not take you serious and end up missing the first party,

but I'll guarantee you they will make it (and only speak English) in order to get to the next party. They do not want to miss out on a party, trust me! (You can also do this with 5 X's, 3 X's or my favorite, if any student in the class speaks their native language the whole class gets an X and after 10 X's there is no party for anyone.)

Younger Classes (Under 10 years old)
1. Teach them simple grammar concepts.
2. Teach the more advanced students verbs and how the tenses change. (past, present, future)
3. Have target sentence patterns outlined in a file. Use this to give yourself target questions to ask your students when playing games or doing activities.
4. Review all vocabulary flashcards as often as possible. Don't just review this week's vocabulary, but continually review all the flashcards you have accumulated throughout the year with your class.
5. Learn about and trace a letter in their letter book. Practice printing or tracing A-Z (big and small letters) on other paper as well. There is no need to push printing too much until your students are old enough to have the coordination to hold a pencil properly. If they are too young, just have them color in the letters.
6. Teach your students about phonics and all the sounds each letter and combination of letters make. The older and more advanced students can start working on short vowel and long vowel sounds.
7. Reviewing vowels. (AEIOU) Print this on the whiteboard. (B _ T) They fill in the sound in the middle when you print the letter A or E or I or O or U. Then print this on the whiteboard. (B _ T E) The silent 'E', then add all vowel sounds again. Now they have to read the word, but it will sound different, it's a long vowel sound.

8. <u>Make or use 'reading word' flashcards for showing your kindergarten students all the new reading words they learn</u>. You can figure out and play lots of games and activities with these cards as well.

9. <u>Many schools will have a weekly poster</u>. Go over and review the new poster a few times each week.

10. <u>Read your class a storybook from your school's collection</u>. Make sure you read them a variety of books, don't always read the same book. Read them every single book you have in your school, and keep reading their favorite books over and over again. Be animated and excited about the book you are reading. Children have great imaginations and love books being read to them.

11. <u>Read their school storybooks</u>. Listen to the CD and discuss the story with them. Also, you can have them read along while using their index finger to follow the words once they get a bit older. Read anything and everything possible. What you see in books, on walls, on the TV, anywhere. Practice reading often.

12. <u>Do some math</u>. Count objects in the room. Print numbers on the whiteboard and have them tell you what number it is. Review counting numbers up to 100 or 1,000. Have them count their tokens for you before they buy a toy with them.

13. <u>Sing songs</u>. Sing their weekly songs and rhymes often. Sing your own songs, any songs, all the songs. Every now and then, stand up, sing and act out a song or two or three or more. Especially, when the class seems to be getting bored, or the kids have been sitting for too long.

14. <u>Go over the 'Classroom Rules' with your kindergarten class regularly</u>.

15. <u>Keep on them with only speaking English</u>. I would give a brand new class up to 6 months before I really start to enforce this rule. But, the earlier you can enforce this rule, the better.

16. <u>Write 100 short storybooks for your students.</u> 'The 100 Storybooks'. Take two pieces of white letter sized paper. Fold in half and put in 3 staples. You now should have a cover page and 7 pages to write a storybook. Along the bottom write the sentence. At the top, draw a picture using crayons. It will take some time, but eventually you will have created 100 children's storybooks with your own personalized sentence structures. Start out with very simple sentence structures and then make them more complicated as you get to 100. Then, make three big posters and put them on the wall. Each poster has all children's names along the top, and thirty three different book titles down the left hand side. One poster will obviously have thirty four books. Now, have each kid in your class read 100 storybooks to get a prize. Make sure you number each storybook and that each storybook corresponds with its title on the poster. This will keep it easy to keep track of them. The students will practice reading the books. When they feel they are ready, have them line up and prove to you that they can read their book. They can read to you or to your co-teacher. If they read it well, they get a happy face in the appropriate square in the grid you have made over the poster. If it was not well read, have the child go and practice again. This project will take a long time to accomplish, so give yourself at least a few months. It is great reading practice and the kids love doing it. They can read 100 storybooks! It is a lot of reading practice for them and builds their confidence.

Classroom Time Structure

Example of a One Hour Class for
Older Students (Over 10 years old)

1. Pre-class. (5 minutes) Check to make sure everyone has completed their homework. Go over any common mistakes that you notice. Quickly re-teach, re-explain, or review the misunderstood concept.

2. Warm-up. (10 minutes) Always start your class with some sort of fun activity or short game. Never start a lesson teaching something new. Review old material and make it extremely simple and fun.

3. Teach something new. (15 minutes) Have the class sit up straight, nothing on their tables, no talking to friends, eyes on the whiteboard, and ears wide open. This is serious time. Now, as clearly and detailed as you can, but in the most simple way possible get your point across and teach your students something new.

4. Do an assignment or activity. (10 minutes) Do an assignment or activity that is related to what you just taught. At first, have the whole class answer your questions at the same time. After they feel more comfortable with the new concept require answers from individual students.

5. Play a game or do something fun. (15 minutes or for the remainder of the class) Do anything that is fun and entertaining. This is the part of class that they all look forward to. This is what they get to do if everyone was well behaved that day and tried their best. If the class

was not good, take this part of class away and give them a writing assignment instead. The last part of class is a reward and make sure you tell them it is a reward. It will possibly be a game, but whatever it is, make sure it is fun. You are still very concerned that they are learning English, so make sure they are still communicating in English too. (Not using their native language)

6. <u>Always assign homework</u>. (The last 5 minutes of class) Give them homework related to today's newly taught lesson. Write the homework on the whiteboard and have them copy it into their homework books.

Example of a 3.5 Hour Morning Class for Younger Students (Under 10 years old)

1. <u>Morning Greeting</u>. (10 minutes) What is the date? Day of week / month / day / year? How is the weather? What did you do yesterday? How are you feeling today and why? Etc.

2. <u>Warm-up</u>. (10 minutes) Review, review, review. Example: Play the hammer game where they need to hit the flashcards. Team A/B or just play for fun and don't keep score.

3. <u>Pass all flashcards around the room</u>. (5 minutes) Each student must say each flashcard as they get passed around to every student.

4. <u>Teach them the new weekly poster</u>. (10 minutes) Have a discussion about the picture, all the weekly new vocabulary (have them repeat each new word 3X), talk about the new sentence structure and anything else that may be on the weekly poster.

5. <u>Make sure everyone has listened to you and have got today's new concept or sentence structure</u>. (2 minutes) Have each child now answer a question to stand up and go line up at the door.

6. Make a good line & go to the bathroom. (5 minutes) Line up and walk to the bathroom singing the weekly song or rhyme. Make sure all the kids wash their hands with soap and water

7. Teach how to do it and then do the book work. (15 minutes) (Example: Pages 3-4). Have everyone sit properly in a semi-circle on the floor in front of your whiteboard. Explain to them how to do the bookwork first, a brief explanation. Once you feel they are ready, let them go to their table and do it for themselves. When they are finished, they put up their hand and you go around checking each child's book in red pen.

8. Come back to the classroom floor and sit down. Play a whiteboard game. (15 minutes) (Example: Play a dice game called 'Snakes and Ladders' on the whiteboard).

9. Have the whole class stand up and sing and act out a few weekly songs and rhymes. (5-10 minutes)

10. Read the class a storybook or two or three. (10 minutes)

11. Make a good line & go to the bathroom again. (5 minutes) Line up and walk to the bathroom singing the weekly song or rhyme. Make sure all the kids wash their hands with soap and water.

12. Come back to class for snack time. (10 minutes) Have all the kids eat their snacks and then come back to sit down on the floor in a semi-circle when they are finished.

13. Everyone stands up and has to answer a question to sit down. (2 minutes)

14. Play Number BINGO. (10 minutes) Have their cards ready for them (photocopy one for each child) and have them color in as you play.

15. Play a game of Pictionary on the whiteboard. Team A/B. (10 minutes)

16. Do their phonics workbook or math workbook. (10-15 minutes) Explain how to do the work and then have

them go and do it themselves. When they are finished their work they can go to playtime.

17. <u>The last 20 minutes of the morning let the children have free time / playtime</u>. (20 minutes) Speaking only in English! (Generally, once a class has been at school for 6 months or longer they are capable of playing in English only)

18. <u>Make a good line & go to the bathroom again</u>. (5 minutes) Line up and walk to the bathroom singing the weekly song or rhyme. Make sure all the kids wash their hands with soap and water.

19. <u>Set up the kids for lunch time</u>. (5 minutes) This is usually when it is time for the native English teacher to go home themselves. Say good-bye to your class and that's it.

20. <u>The whole idea for younger children is to change activities frequently and to keep things simple and fun!</u> It may seem like you are playing a lot of the time, but younger kids are learning way more English than you can imagine when they are playing. Especially when they are listening to the teacher and always communicating in English.

Games

Quick Games

1. **A quick note about games.** (2 big dice, a sticky ball, 2 toy hammers, a ball, some magnets, and lots of scrap paper are all props that a teacher should carry with them or at least have available at their school) I try to explain all these games in the best way I know how. But, if one of them doesn't quite make sense to you or you can come up with an idea on how to expand on a game or take something away from the game; that is ok. Be creative, innovative and have your own style on how you play these games. Some of these games I describe as Team A/B. But, they could also be played as individual games. Some games say there is a winner, but sometimes you can play the same game just for fun where nobody is the winner. Sometimes you can play a game to 8, sometimes to 10, sometimes to 15, and sometimes just play the game until a certain time. In general, the younger the students are, the more simplified you will have to make the game or activity. The older and more advanced students will want more complex and sophisticated games and activities. There are many variations that can be done to most of the games mentioned here.

2. **2 lines / quickest sits.** (No props needed) Have all your students line up in two lines down the middle of the classroom and ask the first two students in line a question. The first one to answer your question correctly gets to stay in the game and go to the back of the line.

The loser has to go sit down. The last student standing is the winner.

3. **Stand up, answer a question to sit down.** (No props needed) Have all students in the class stand up. Ask them a question, or have them ask you a question to sit down. That's it.

4. **Quick version of Pictionary.** (No props needed) Just draw pictures on the whiteboard and your students try to guess what you are drawing.

5. **What is missing?** (A few flashcards). Put some flashcards up on the whiteboard and review them with your class. Then, take one away without anyone seeing which one you took. Now, the children need to figure out what card is missing? The first student to put their hand up and tell you the answer is the winner.

6. **Hangman.** (No props needed) Draw a hanging device on the whiteboard, then think up of a sentence you want the children to guess at. Example: The ball is on the table. Draw a line under each letter that would be there, but don't write the letters or the words, the students have to guess at that. Example: _ _ _   _ _ _ _   _ _   _ _   _   _ _   _ _ _ _ _. Now ask a child in the class to guess a letter. If they get it right, write it on the line. If the letter is not on the board, you draw a face on the hanging device, then an arm, then other arm, then leg, then other leg, then eyes, then nose and if you get to mouth, they lose, they hung themselves. If they can guess the sentence before they hang themselves, everyone in the class is the winner. For older students, you can ask a student to come up and play the hangman game for you. They decide on the sentence and they lead the game and ask other students in the class to guess. You just sit to the side and monitor making sure all communication is being done in English.

7. **Tic-tac-toe.** (No props needed) Team A/B or Team Teacher / Students. You make a grid on the whiteboard containing 9 squares. You ask your class if they want to be team 'X' or 'O', you become the opposite team. Have one student come up and place an X in a square, then you put an O, then they put and X, then you put an 0 etc. The team who can get 3 in a row either horizontally, vertically, or diagonally is the winner. Remember, if the teacher loses it is always funny. Tell your class that you never lose, that you are the best X's and O's player around. Then, when you lose, they will laugh extra hard.

8. **Make words games.** (Some scrap paper) Write a small grid on the whiteboard with letters in it. Put around 8 letters in it, including a couple vowels. Put your class into groups and see how many words they can come up with by only using these letters. Have them print their answers on a scrap piece of paper. The person or group with the most words spelled correctly is the winner.

9. **Bigger or smaller.** (2 big dice) Choose a middle number of 6. Now, go around the classroom and have each student roll both dice. Each student must decide if they will roll higher or lower than the number 6. They roll and if they are correct, they don't have to answer a question. If they are incorrect, they must answer a question or do whatever English chore you have for them. If they tie, roll a 6, they must roll again.

10. **0-10 or 0-100 or 0-1,000 or 0-10,000.** (Some scrap paper) For 0-100, choose a number between 0-100 and write it on a piece of paper, then hide it in your pocket. Write the number 100 at the top of the whiteboard with a big arrow pointing down. Write a 0 at the bottom on the whiteboard with a big arrow pointing up. Make a blank square in the middle. Go around the classroom one student at a time and have them guess what number is in your pocket. When they say a number, erase the

current number on the whiteboard and replace it with their number. They will now see that they have to go higher or lower. Eventually, they will get it narrowed down enough to figure out the number you have in your pocket. The student who guesses the correct number first is the winner.

Whiteboard Games

1. **How to play whiteboard games.** First, you set up the game and you play the game as it would normally be played out. Then, before a student can take their turn at the game, they must answer an English question that the teacher gives them. When that student answers the question, their whole team can repeat the answer again. The opposing team just listens to the answer being repeated. You are playing a game, but you are also practicing all sorts of target sentence structures as you play.

2. **Snakes & Ladders.** (A big die, two magnets) Team A/B. Draw a snakes & ladders board on the whiteboard. It is a grid of 50 or more squares. Use a black marker for the squares and numbering, a red marker for the snakes, and a blue marker for the ladders. The first team to the top corner square is the winner.

3. **Sneaky Snail.** (A big die, 2 magnets) Team A/B. Put your marker in the middle of the whiteboard and start drawing a line spiraling to the left. Keep spiraling further and further outwards until you take up most of whiteboard. Now, make an end to your spiral by closing it off. Draw a long snail's neck up the left side with a round head, smiling face and antennas to make the whole thing look like a snail with a big shell. Now, divide up the snail's shell into 25-30 small squares and number them. The first team to get out of the snail is the winner.

4. **Shark Game.** (A big die, 2 magnets) Team A/B or Team Teacher / Students. Draw a long ladder going across some water with sharks swimming in it. Some of the rings on the ladder have no line on the bottom, a hole in the square. If a team rolls the die and ends up on a square with nothing there, they fall into the water and get eaten by the sharks. That team needs to start from the beginning again. The first team to climb over to the other side of the water and not fall in it is the winner.

5. **Climb the stairs.** (A big die, two magnets) Team A/B. Draw a tall set of stairs on the whiteboard. The first team to the top is the winner.

6. **Climb the tree.** (A big die, 2 magnets) Team A/B. Draw two trees on the whiteboard. Write the numbers up to 20 on each tree trunk. The first team to the top of their tree is the winner. You can also draw some red apples on your tree to make it look more appealing.

7. **Climb the hills.** (A big die, 2 magnets) Team A/B. Draw a few different towers on the whiteboard. The first tower is 2 squares tall, the next tower is 3 squares tall, and the last tower is 4 squares tall. A team member rolls the die and needs to roll at least that high of a number to get over each particular tower. If they do, they get to go again and try the next tower. If they roll less, they are stuck behind the tower and lose their turn. The first team to clear all towers is the winner.

8. **Pirate.** (A big die, 2 magnets) Team A/B. Draw a squared off pyramid on the whiteboard with a flag at the top of it. The pyramid should not be a straight line to the top, it should be going up like a set of stairs on either side. The first team to get up to the flag is winner.

9. **Snake game.** (A big die, 2 magnets) Team A/B. Draw a long snake on the whiteboard. Make many different square sections on the snake. Number the squares from

1 to 20. The tail is 1, the head is 20. The first team to race their magnet through the snake is the winner.

10. **Walk the plank.** (A big die, 2 magnets) Team A/B or Team Teacher / Students. Draw a ship in the middle of the whiteboard with a plank going off to the side. Have the plank broken up into squares and print on numbers up to 20. Draw sharks swimming in the water. Each team rolls the die and they get closer and closer to the edge. The first team to roll the die and go too far, fall into the water is the loser. Or have each team roll to move the other team's magnet. Therefore, make sure when a team rolls the die, that they know they are not rolling for themselves to move, they are moving their opponents off the plank.

11. **Turtle & Hare.** (A big die, 2 magnets) Team A/B. First, draw a line across your whiteboard and number it 1 to 20. This will be the racing line. Put a grid up in the corner of your whiteboard. Have A B C D along the top, and have 1 2 3 4 down the side. You also make this grid on a scrap piece of paper in your pocket. On the grid in your pocket you have different values such as (+2) (-1) (+4) (0) etc. Now, when a student answers a question, they get to choose a square, their team gets to move that far forward or backwards along the racing line. The first team to the finish line is the winner.

12. **Fishing in a boat game.** (A big die, 9 to 15 magnets) Team A/B. Draw two boats floating in the water on the whiteboard, one boat for each team. Place an uneven number of magnets throughout the water. These magnets represent fish. At the bottom of each boat have a 3 step ladder. Number it, 1 2 3. Now, when a team rolls the die, they can reel in that many fish. But, it is a 3 step process to catch each fish. The team who catches the most fish is the winner.

13. **Throw sticky ball at a target on the whiteboard.** (1 sticky ball) Team A/B. Draw a bulls-eye target on the whiteboard. Or make any design you wish for the students to hit. Usually just 3 different sized circles on the whiteboard. The middle circle is 5 points, second circle is 2 points, and the outside circle is 1 point. Pick a spot to throw from and make an imaginary line there. Go through each team twice. The team with the most points wins. Or have each individual student answer a question to throw the ball. Have just one target. If they hit that target, that student wins the small prize, a token or something.

14. **Squares game.** (No props needed) Team A/B. Draw a large amount of dots on the whiteboard in a square grid pattern. When a student answers an English question correctly, they get to draw a line between any two of the dots. They only get to draw one line, unless the current line they just drew completes a square, then this team gets to draw another line. If they complete another square, they can go again and again until they don't complete a square anymore. Once a student completes a square, they can write their team A or B in the middle. The team that ends up with the most squares is the winner. If a small class, you may also play, but each student writes their name in the square instead of the team. The student with the most squares is the winner.

15. **4X's 4 O's.** (No props needed) Team X/O. Simply draw a large square grid on the whiteboard like a chess board. When a team answers a question correctly, they come up and draw an X or an O. The first team to complete 4 X's or 4 O's up or down or on a diagonal is the winner. Make sure you draw a very large grid with many squares.

16. **Write different words all over the whiteboard.** Team A/B. One student from each team comes up to the front. You say a word and the first player to slap that word with

their hand wins a point for their team. The first team to get to a pre-determined score is the winner. The first team to 10 wins.

17. **Play the boom-boom game.** (Prepare a boom-boom game card before class) Team A/B. Draw a square grid on the whiteboard, A B C D E along the top, 1 2 3 4 5 down the side. Keep the squares blank for now, but on your piece of paper draw the same grid, but on yours draw: a gun, 2 guns, a cross, 2 crosses and a bomb. When a student chooses a square: If a gun: They can tell a person on the other team to stand up. 2 guns: Choose 2 people to stand up. If a cross: It's an ambulance symbol, they can choose a person on their team to sit down. 2 crosses: Choose 2 people to sit down. If a bomb: The person who is answering the question must stand up. When all players on one team are standing up, that team loses. Make sure they stand up properly behind their chair to make this game the most fun.

More Games

1. **Build two towers.** (A lot of fairly big square blocks) Team A/B. After each team answers a question correctly they can put up a block on their tower. Keep building the blocks higher and higher, and keep asking more and more English questions until one of the towers falls down. That team is the loser. Or you can just build one tower for the game.

2. **Two chairs at the front game.** (2 chairs) Team A/B. One student from each team comes to the front and sits in a chair with their back to the whiteboard. You print a word or draw a picture on the whiteboard. The whole class needs to verbally describe this word to the two students at the front without saying the actual word. The first student at the front who guesses the word gets a point for their team. If the team describing the word

accidently says the word, the other team gets the point. If no one can guess the word after 1 minute, no team gets a point. Move on to the next word and the next two students.

3. **Give many balls game.** (About 50 balls, a basket or bucket) Team A/B or every student is their own team. Have 50 questions ready to ask your class at a very quick pace. You just go around the classroom and when a student answers a question correctly, they get a ball. The more questions a student answers, the more balls that student gets. After you give out all the balls to the class. Ask one student at a time to come up to the front and try and throw their balls into a basket. Each ball they get in the basket = 1 point or 1 token. The more questions a student answered, the more chances for rewards that student has.

4. **Relay spelling game.** (2 markers or chalk and a chalk board is even better) Team A/B. Have your students lined up in two lines in front of the whiteboard. You say one of their spelling words. Each student at the front of the line writes one letter on the board, then passes the marker back to the next student and goes to the back of the line. The next student prints the second letter in the word etc. The first team to spell the word correctly gets a point for their team. Then, do the next word. Keep going until one team completes a certain amount of words, that team is the winner. Tell your students to be careful not to get the tip of the marker on other students clothes when passing the marker back to the next student during the relay race.

5. **Laughing game.** (No props needed) Team A/B. Choose one student from each class to come to the front of the room. You have one student ask a student on the opposite team a question. But, this student tries to be funny and make the other student laugh. Give 10 seconds for each

try. If the student laughs, the opposite team gets a point. If they don't laugh, then this team gets the point. Then, you move on to the next two students and so on. The first team to 5 points is the winner.

6. **Play ghostbusters.** (A soft paper bat, a bunch of flashcards) Get everyone to sit in a circle on the floor. Give every student a flashcard and have them hold it in front of them with the picture facing forward. Now, you choose one student and give them a soft and safe bat to use. That student will be standing in the middle of the circle. When you call out a flashcard the student in the middle must hit the flashcard you call out before the student with the flashcard calls out a different flashcard. When a student's flashcard is called. That student must quickly say another flashcard before they get hit. If they get hit, they are the new batter. The student in the middle keeps going around and around until eventually they hit a flashcard before that student says a different flashcard. Sounds confusing, but actually a very simple and fun game to play.

7. **Heart attack.** (A large amount of flashcards) Team A/B. Two players from each team come up to the front table and you start flipping through flashcards saying each flashcard out loud as you flip them. If you say the word that is on the flashcard, then the two students don't do anything, they don't hit the flashcard, they just wait. When you say a word that is not on the flashcard, then both students must hit the flashcard. The first hand on the flashcard is the winner. Also, if a student hits the flashcard when they are not supposed to, they lose a point for their team.

8. **Hotter / warmer / colder game.** (An object) Show your whole class some fairly big object. Have one of your students leave the classroom and then hide the object. When that student comes back inside, nobody can tell

them where the object is. They can only say "hotter" which is very close to it, "warmer" which is getting closer to it, "colder" which is getting farther away from it. The student takes the clues and tries to locate the object as fast as possible.

9. **<u>Each student draws a letter with their index finger on the back of the student in front of them</u>.** (No props needed) Team A/B. Have the students stand in two lines in the middle of your classroom. The lines will need to be even, if not then the teacher should join at the back of one of the teams to make sure it is two evenly numbered lines. Tell or show the two people at the back of each line a letter. When you say "go", the two students at the back of the line print with their finger on the back of the student in front of them who needs to figure out what letter it is. Then, they write on the back of the student in front of them etc. until the student at the front on the line gets it. The front student needs to print that letter on the whiteboard. The first team to do this successfully gets a point for their team.

10. **Categories.** (Give both teams at least 2 whiteboard markers each) Team A/B. Split the whiteboard into two parts by drawing a big line down the middle. Each team has to write down as many words in whatever category you give them. Such as food, animals, people or whatever you want. The team that has the most words for their category with the correct spelling after 3 minutes is the winner.

11. **Disaster.** (No props needed) Team A/B. One team goes outside the classroom and the other team stays inside the classroom. Have every child inside the classroom change one thing around. Turn something upside down, move something from here to there, put a chair on the desk etc. The other team comes inside and needs to guess what was changed. For each thing they guess, they get a point for

their team. After a certain time limit, time is up, and the teams need to reverse roles. The inside team now goes outside and the outside team comes inside. The team with the most points is the winner. Tell the children to keep the changes easy and don't change something too miniscule or difficult. Also, make sure that any and all changes are visible. Don't allow the students to fully hide something. Or you can also have all the children leave the classroom, and the teacher changes one thing for each of the number of students in their class. Then, the teacher leaves the classroom and the children change one thing each.

12. **Play Ghost.** (No props needed) You ask one student to leave the classroom and choose one student in the classroom to be 'it'. That student in the classroom can start making movements or actions. Clapping their hands, shaking their head, doing something funny, whatever etc. Everyone in the classroom follows and copies exactly what the leader is doing. The person who was outside comes inside now and has to try and guess who the leader is. The leader in the classroom changes movements often to give the guesser a chance to see who this leader is. See how many guesses it takes the guesser to figure out who the leader is.

13. **Play wink.** (A chair for each child) Have all students sit in a circle on chairs or they can sit on the floor. Choose one child to go outside. Choose one child in the room to be the winker. Tell the child from outside to come in now. That child must figure out who the winker is, but no one can tell them. All students need to be told to keep looking around the room at each other. The winker looks around the room as well and when they wink at another student, that student must pretend to get hit and fall to the floor. See how long it takes the student who went outside to figure out who is the winker is.

14. **Play Number BINGO, Word BINGO, or Phonics BINGO.** (Make a BINGO sheet or have your students make their own on a scrap piece of paper). Draw a square grid pattern on the paper so there are five columns and five rows for a total of twenty five squares. Then, have the students print the #'s 1-25 anywhere they want. (Number BINGO) Or write out 25 recent spelling words in any square they choose. (Word BINGO) Or use 25 different phonics sounds and have them write those anywhere they want. (Phonics BINGO) You should already have your own sheet with the numbers, words, or phonic sounds on it. Cut your 25 squares out and mix up the squares and put inside a basket or something. You take one square at a time and call out to the class what it is. The students color in their square with a crayon as you call it. The first player to get a line either horizontally, vertically, or diagonally and also the first player who shouts "BINGO!" is the winner. You can also make the game last longer by asking your students to get 2 lines or 3 lines before they can win and shout "BINGO!"

15. **Write 20 answers to 20 questions correctly game.** (The teacher writes out 20-30 questions on 20-30 different pieces of scrap paper) Divide the class into small teams of 2-3 people per team. You sit at the front of the class an equal distance away from each team. Each team must take one question at a time and bring it back to their table. They write the answer to the question and line up in single file in front of you. You mark the question, if the sentence is the correct grammar with period and capital letter, then write that group's name on the scrap paper and give them another question. If incorrect, tell them what to fix and they must bring the question all the way back to their table, correct it, and line back up to show you the correct answer. Once all question papers are handed out, count up how many each group

completed. The team who answered the most questions is the winner.

16. **Play 20 Questions.** (You will need a lot of small rewards or tokens) Choose one student to come to the front and print a word down on a piece of paper, nobody else knows what it is, except the teacher who knows what it is in order to help with answering questions and keeping the flow of the game. The rest of the class asks questions to try and figure out what the word is. Example: Is it a thing or an animal? What color is it? Is it big or small? Is it in your house? Is it in this classroom? Etc. Each student gets one token for asking a question. If they just go for the answer, that is not considered a question worth getting a token, but is just a guess at the answer. If they are wrong, they don't get a token, but it still counts as asking one question of the 20. They have up to 20 questions to figure out the word. If a student guesses the correct word, they win 5 tokens. If no one can guess the word after 20 questions the student at the front who wrote the word wins the 5 tokens. Don't allow the student to use such a hard word that the class might not even know what it is. Tell them to keep it somewhat simple and the game will be more fun for everyone.

17. **Play Pictionary.** (No props needed) Team A/B. One student comes up for each team one at a time. They draw a picture of what you tell them, or they can choose their own picture. Or the teacher can draw the pictures for them, the students just guess. The first team to guess what it is gets a point for their team. The first team to 10 is the winner.

18. **Play a simple version of Jeopardy.** (Have a Jeopardy board already made up on a scrap piece of paper with your questions written on it) Team A/B. Have 6 different categories and 4 different questions in each category. $100, $200, $300, $400 in each category. The more

money the question is, the harder the question should be. Examples that a category can be is food, clothing, family, verbs, spelling, geography, etc. One player on the team chooses a category and value, but anyone on that team can answer the question. If that team can't correctly answer the question in 1 minute, the other team can have a chance to answer the question and steal the money. The team who earns the most money is the winner.

19. **Play a game of Yahtzee.** (Give your students a piece of scrap paper so they can keep track of their own yahtzee score card, 5 dice, a shaking cup) Play the game in a simplified version, by just using the numbers 1-6. The score is added up by seeing how many 1's they can roll, then how many 2's, in any order up to 6 different turns in total. Within the turn, each child gets to roll 5 dice 3 different times, then record their score. This means each child will have 6 turns each. The player who rolls the highest score of all their rolls combined is the winner. Example: player rolls 3 2's = 6 points, player rolls 4 6's = 24 points etc.

20. **Stella Ella Olla.** (No props needed) Sit in a circle facing inwards either on the floor or in chairs. Everyone sits with theirs palms upwards facing outward. Everyone's right hand is on top, everyone's left hand is under the person's hand beside them. Sing the song as you pick up your right hand and clap the person's hand to the left of you. You choose one person to start and everyone claps along to the beat. You keep singing the song, and they keep hitting the next person's hand until, on the # 5. That person must hit the hand of the person beside them to stay in the game and the person they hit is out. If the person going for the hit misses, because the person's hand who was supposed to be hit, moved it out of the way, which is allowed, then the person missing the hit is out of the game. You keep going and more and more people

get eliminated, until you have just the one winner. Here is the song... Stella ella olla clap, clap, clap. Sing 'S' jeeko jeeko, jeeko jeeko jack. Sing, 'S' jeeko, jeeko. Sing 1, 2, 3, 4, 5!

21. **Play UNO cards.** (You should be able to buy UNO cards from any international English toy store). Just take a break in class one day and sit around playing UNO. Or let the kids play UNO on their break-time. Don't forget when a student has only one card left, they must say "UNO". If that student forgets and another students notices by saying so, the player who forgot to say "UNO" needs to pick up 3 more cards. The first player to get rid of all their cards is the winner. Further instructions come with the cards. This is a very fun card game that many children love to play.

22. **Play go fish.** (Use a normal deck of playing cards). Have everyone sit in a circle around a big table. Deal out four to six cards to each of the students. Put the rest of the cards upside down in the center of the table. Then, go around the room in order. Each student needs to ask any other student they want if they have a particular card number. If yes, that student takes the card off the other student and gets to go again. They display their pair on the table. Once they ask a student and that student doesn't have a card, their turn is over. That other player will say "go fish" and the first student must take a card from the middle. The play continues around the room one student at a time. One side note, if a student takes a card from the middle and it makes them the pair they were originally asking for. They just say "fish, fish, got my wish." Then, they still get to go again. Play until all the cards are matched up. The player with the most pairs is the winner.

23. **Play a game of Chess.** (A chess board and pieces) One on one game only. If you have time, sit around and play

a game of chess with a child. Or just leave a chessboard in your classroom and they can play on breaks or when they have free time.

Games For Younger Children (Under 10 years old)

1. **Hammer game.** (2 hammers, some English flashcards to hit) Team A/B. Spread about 6 to 8 flashcards on the floor or on a sturdy table. Have one player from each team come to the front and grab a hammer. There teacher says what flashcard to hit and the first student to hit that flashcard gets a point for their team. Two new students come up to the front and the game goes on and on like this. Play up to 10 points.

2. **Throw a ball into a bucket or basket.** (A ball, a bucket or basket) Team A/B. Have a throwing line that the students throw from. The first team to 5 wins or just keep playing as long as you want and the team with the most points wins. For a more complicated version, you can have them choose a line to throw from. Make them farther and farther back. The farthest line is worth 5 points, the closest line is worth only 1 point. Lines 5, 4, 3, 2, 1. They can choose which line they want to gamble from, how many points they want to get, but the more points they want, the harder the shot will be to make. The team with the most points is the winner.

3. **Play spin.** (New weekly flashcards, a big die) Write the numbers 1-6 on the whiteboard. Have one student roll the die and the whole class must say the flashcard you're holding that many times. But, if it is #1 they must stand up, turn around and sit down. If it is #6 they must stand up, jump 3 times then sit down. The last student to complete the task of #1 or #6 is the loser and must stand up and answer the teacher's English question or do an English chore.

4. **Play hot potato.** (A ball or soft object, an electronic music device) Have the children sit in a circle on the floor or on chairs. Have them pass a ball around while the music is on. When the music stops, the student who has the ball or last touched the ball if the ball flies off somewhere is the loser. This student is out of the circle. Keep playing and eliminating children until you get down to the winner. Or the loser has to stand up and answer 2 or 3 English questions from the teacher. Then, they can sit back into the circle and play again.

5. **A-Z race.** (2 exact same sets of flashcards with the same letters A-Z on them) Team A/B. Each team scrambles their flashcards into a big mix up. You say "go". The first team to put the alphabet in order is the winner. You can do this with uppercase or lowercase lettering.

6. **Upper / Lower case matching of the letters A-Z.** (A set of flashcards from A-Z) Team A/B. Have one child from each team come to the front. Show them or draw on the whiteboard an upper case letter. They both have to race to see who can find the matching lower case letter the fastest. That student gets a point for their team. The first team to 10 is the winner.

7. **Cowboy game.** (A few different flashcards) Team A/B. One player from each team comes to the middle of the classroom standing back to back. You give each student a flashcard. They walk 3 paces in the opposite direction of each other. Then, the teacher says "turn around". The first student to see and say the other student's flashcard is the winner or gets a point for their team.

8. **Musical chairs.** (one chair for each child, music, a CD player) Have all the children sit in a circle on chairs with their chair facing outwards. When you play music all children must stand up and move around the circle in the same direction. Take away one chair each time or two chairs each time if the class is very big. When the music

stops, all the children scramble to find a chair to sit down on. The student who does not have a chair is out of the game. Eventually you are down to one chair and two students. The student that manages to sit down in the chair first when the final music stops is the winner.

9. **Play dodgeball.** (Use a very light blown up air ball, a very large open area either outside at a park or inside) Team A/B. Be extra careful, this game can become dangerous if your students are not in control of themselves. You have a line down the middle and half the students on either side of the line. You throw in a ball or sometimes 2 balls. Without crossing the line the students must throw the ball back and forth at each other. If a student gets hit by a ball, they are out of the game. But, they can catch the ball. If a student catches the ball, they are still safe. Keep playing until all players on one team are eliminated. The team with players still standing is the winner.

10. **Two cars racing game.** (2 cars that a student can fit in and ride or 2 tricycles) Team A/B. Make a circular obstacle track for the students to race around. Have an even amount of players on each team. Two students start on the starting line as you say "go". They race around the track. Even have them do other chores while finishing the track, like take a ball and put it into the basket, crawl under a table etc. Then, when they are finished the track, the next student goes. The first team to finish all their riders is the winner.

11. **Red light / Green Light.** (A large area either inside or outside) Have all your students go to one side of the room. The teacher stays at the other end facing them. When the teacher says "green light" all the students can walk towards the teacher, no running. When the teacher says "red light" all the students must stop. If anyone continues to move forward, make too much noise, or fall off their stance, they are out and must go sit down. The

first student to make their way all the way to the teacher is the winner. Then. Tell them all to go back and do it again.

12. **What time is it Mr. Wolf?** (One very large area either inside or outside). Have all the students except one go to the one side of the play area. They are the pigs. One student goes to the opposite side of the room. That student is the wolf. All the pigs say "What time is it Mr. Wolf?" The wolf makes up a fake time, say 2 O'clock or 5 O'clock etc. The pigs must walk that many steps towards the wolf, then stop and ask again "What time is it Mr. Wolf?" Finally, when the wolf answers "It's lunch time". The wolf turns around and chases after the pigs. The pigs need to run back to the other side of the play area before the wolf touches them. If they get touched, they turn into a wolf also. You play again and again. Each time you get more and more wolves. Play until you have so many wolves that there are no more pigs left to catch.

13. **Sleeping horse.** (No props needed) Have all the children lie on the floor with their legs bent up like a triangle, but their hands straight up in the air. They need to lie as still as they can. They can't move or talk or laugh. If they do talk or laugh or move, they are out. The students who can lie the stillest and quietest the longest are the winners. An excellent game to cool down an overly excited kindergarten class.

14. **Split your class into two groups and have them sing one of their weekly songs or rhymes.** (No props needed) It's a competition. You are the judge to decide which group sang better. Which group was loud, but was not screaming. Which group was the clearest, not mumbling etc. This group will be the winner. Give them a small reward.

Activities

Quick Activities

1. **Pass flashcards around the classroom.** (A lot of flashcards) Take all the flashcards you have accumulated so far in your class. Just start at one side of your classroom if your students are sitting at desks, or have all your students come and sit in a circle. Hand the first student a flashcard and say what it is, each next student also must say what it is. They must also say what it is out loud and pass it on to the next student. As they do this, you hand them another flashcard, and another and another etc. If they don't know what it is, they have to ask their friend or teacher before they can pass it along. Keep saying and handing out flashcards all around the room until all your flashcards are gone.

2. **Theme ball.** (A ball) Choose a theme, say food for instance. Now throw a ball back and forth from student to teacher, student to teacher over and over again. But, each time a student or teacher gets the ball, they must say a word from that theme. Example: They must say "pizza" and then throw it back to you, you say "hamburger" and throw it to a different child who says "apple", who throws it back etc. Each time you play this game, change the theme. If a child drops the ball, they must stand up and answer 3 questions or do an English chore specified by the teacher.

3. **Throw a student the ball if they get the right answer.** (A ball) In this activity, it is a reward to get the ball and

to throw the ball. Just go around the classroom asking each student a question. If they can give you the correct answer using the correct grammar, then throw them the ball. They get to catch it and throw it back to you. Move on to another student, and so on.

4. **Wordsnake.** (No props needed) Write a word on the top left corner on the whiteboard with a dash next to the word. Your students have to come up with more and more words for you to snake along. You keep printing them on the whiteboard and they keep shouting out words for you to print. The last letter of the previous word needs to be the first letter in the next word. Example: pig – girl – lion – name – elephant etc. Once all words are on the whiteboard, use your finger to guide them along as you read out each word as a class. If your class is advanced enough, have them stand up and put a word or two or three into a sentence before they can sit down.

5. **First student to put this word into a sentence wins.** (No props needed) You tell the class a certain sentence structure. Explain to them they must make their sentence in this way. Example: Past Continuous: Yesterday, I was riding my bike. Choose two students to come to the front of the class. You say a word, any word. The first student to make a correct sentence is the winner. Don't let them say easily made sentences like I want a… or I like a… Make sure they make a target sentence as it makes the game more challenging and fun.

6. **Come to the front and answer 3 questions before you can sit down.** (No props needed) Or you can have each student print 3 questions each on a piece of paper. You check each question for grammar mistakes. If incorrect, tell them what to change, go back to their seat, change it and bring it back to you. Soon, you will have a collection of questions. Now, go around the room and ask one question at a time to one student at a time. Or you

can now use these questions to play a different game or activity.

7. **Answer a question or ask the teacher a question to go home.** (No props needed) Or to enter the classroom or to go on break etc.

8. **Take today's new vocabulary and make a funny sentence.** (No props needed) Show the next student a new word and have them put that word into a sentence as you move around the classroom selecting the next student and so on.

9. **Take all of today's new vocabulary and have your students write a sentence for each new word.** (No props needed) They can write them in their notebooks or on a scrap piece of paper. One sentence for each new word. Put a square around the new word.

10. **True / False.** (No props needed) The teacher stands at the front of the class and says a statement. Go around to each student one at a time and have them figure out if the statement is true or false. Example: My father lives on the moon. If they are correct, they can win a small reward or token. Keep going around the classroom and keep making different true or false statements as many times as you want. Or you can also play this game in Team A/B. Split your class into two halves. Go around and say statements. If they are correct they get a point, if they are incorrect they get no point. The team with the most points is the winner.

11. **Roll a big die, say left or right.** (A big die). Start at one student in the class and work your way around the classroom. Give that student a die and let them choose left or right, then they throw the die onto the floor. The number the die is showing, you count that many students over and make them stand up. Ask them a English question or have them complete whatever English task

you have planned. Now, it is their turn to throw the die and say left or right. Keep going and playing the game.

12. **Hide three objects in your classroom and have the students go and find them.** (Any 3 objects you can find) The students who find the three objects are the winners.

13. **I spy with my little eye.** (No props needed) The teacher sits at the front of the class and says "I spy with my little eye, something that is… blue, or big, or round, or square, or something that is on the window etc. Keep giving the children hints until they figure out what you are looking at, spying on.

14. **Riddles. What am I?** (No props needed) Choose to be anything you want. Then, start giving clues to what you are. It becomes a riddle for you students to try and figure out. The first person to guess what you are is the winner.

More Activities

1. **Unscramble sentences on the whiteboard.** (No props needed) Write each sentence in the wrong order and have your class figure out the correct order. Or make a common grammatical error with each sentence and see if you class can spot them.

2. **Write 5 to 10 questions on the whiteboard.** (No props needed) Your students answer on scrap paper or in their workbook. If they write the correct answer with correct grammar and use a capital letter and period, they are finished. If you find any mistakes, show them and have them go back to their seat and correct them. Once everyone in the class is finished, move on to your next activity.

3. **Write a story on the whiteboard and have your students read it.** (No props needed) For less advanced students, just think of a very easy story to print on the whiteboard.

You can draw some pictures to go with it too. For more advanced students, you can have them help you create the story and tell you what to write. Go around the room one by one. Each student must make at least one sentence in the story. Then, when you are finished, using your finger as a guide have all the students read the story along with you. Then, you can just erase the story and forget about it, move on to something different.

4. **Read your class a story or make up a story and tell them.** (No props needed) Make up a story if you have to and try to make it funny if you can. Then, after you tell them the story they can answer questions on it. Write questions for them to answer in their notebooks or just have a class discussion after you tell them the story.

5. **Play Teacher Says.** (No props needed) This is a very popular game. The teacher stands at the front and tells the students what to do. All the students have to do what the teacher says, if the teachers says "teacher says" before he says to do it. Example: "Teacher says touch your head." Then, all students touch their head. Then, when the teacher doesn't say "teacher says". Example: "Touch your head." The students do not touch their heads. They only do things when the teacher says "teacher says" first. If a student makes a mistake or takes too long to follow your command is out of the game and must sit down. The remaining students standing are the winners.

6. **Charades.** (No props needed) Have one student come to the front and act like something, such as an animal. They act it out, while the rest of the class tries to figure out what they are. The student that guesses first is the winner. Now, that student can become the new actor if they wish or you will need to choose another student to become the actor.

7. **Play telephone game.** (No props needed) The teacher makes up a fairly long sentence. Have all the children

sit in a semi-circle. Then, ask a child to go outside the classroom and tell them the sentence. That student must come back inside and whisper it to the first child who whispers it on to the next etc. All the way around the circle until the last student stands up and goes to the front to say the sentence. It will often be way different and totally wrong. That is ok, this is the funny part about the activity.

8. **Clapping 3's.** (No props needed) Have the whole class stand in a circle. You start going around the circle having each student counting from 1 up. 1, 2, 3, 4, 5, 6, etc. But, every 3rd number can't be said, it must be clapped. They clap their own hands together. Keep going as high as you can. When a student makes a mistake, they are out of the game. Start over from 1 when a student is eliminated, the last one standing is the winner.

9. **Draw a square grid pattern on the whiteboard.** (No props needed) Example: Print I / He / She on the left side, and on the top print school, box, and car. Use a magnet and put it in any square you wish. The class has to come up with and say whatever sentence you have given them combined with what words the magnet is showing to use. You can apply this activity to a lot of the other games you play in class also. Or you can just have the whole class stand up and say a sentence structure to sit down.

10. **Play an activity called 'stop'.** (No props needed) You tell a story from your past or make up a fake, funny story. This can also come from when you are reading a story, or just when you are talking in general with the class. The students will listen carefully to what you are saying. When they hear you say a word that they don't know, someone will say "stop!" out loud. If most of the class agrees that they don't know this word either, the student who yelled "stop!" first gets a reward. If everyone else

in the class already knows it, nobody gets a reward, just review what the word means and move on. Keep track of these newly learned words in a book, file or poster. Then, you can use these words for review games or activities.

11. **The Secret Box.** (A box, 15-20 different easily recognizable objects to put into the box). The teacher stands at the front of the class and takes each object out 1 by 1 showing and explaining to the children what each one is. After you finish doing this, put all the objects back into the box so no one can see them. Now, go around the class and see who can remember what is inside the box. Can they remember them all? What objects did they forget about?

12. **Tape a piece of paper on the back of each student**. (a piece of paper for each child with a noun printed on it, some tape) Each piece of paper has a noun on it, and you tape one of these on each student's back. They cannot see what word they are. Your students must figure out what they are by going around the room and asking questions to their friends. But, their friend cannot tell them the answer, each student needs to figure it out on their own by asking more and more questions and narrowing it down. See how long it takes for everyone to figure out what they are.

13. **Make a directions sheet.** (Take a blank piece of paper and write out as many directions as you can think of, photocopy one copy for every student in your class). Hand out this paper to every student in the class. The students start at #1 and follow the directions all the way to the end. Example: #1 - Write your name on the whiteboard. #2 - Go to the office and read one storybook. #3 - Write the alphabet on the back on this paper. Etc. The longer you can make this activity last, the better. So, think of some good directions.

14. **Let them be the teacher for 5 minutes, you sit down and be one of the students.** (No props needed) They can lead any number of simple games or activities you have taught them and they are familiar with. Example: Let them lead hangman, wordsnake, tic-tack-toe etc.

15. **Do a word search.** (Photocopies of the word search for each child) There are quite a few websites online that will do everything for you. You just type in your words and hit create, then print, it's very easy.

16. **Write notes or letters to each other in class.** (some scrap paper) Create some sort of organized plan to exchange notes with their friends.

17. **Have a spelling test just for fun.** (No props needed) Have each student exchange their test with the student to their left. Now, you can take up the test as a whole class and let your students mark it.

18. **Phonics drilling.** (No props needed) Print all the phonics sounds you can think of on the whiteboard. Start at one side of the classroom and go around. Have each student one at a time say to you what the phonics sound is that you are pointing at.

19. **Review verbs.** (No props needed) Have each student in the class make a sentence. Change the tense from past simple to past continuous to present simple to present continuous to future simple to future continuous. Or just have them tell you the past to present to future. Or just have them tell you the past.

20. **Have a debate / argument on any topic.** (No props needed) Split the class into two groups. One half argues for a particular issue and the other half argues against a particular issue. After the argument is settled, have each group change their argument, so they get a chance to argue for both sides of the issue. Example: English is good / bad, school is fun / boring, candy is good for you / bad for you. When it is all over and done have them

write you a short essay on how they truly feel about the issue.

21. **Have the class conduct interviews with each other.** (No props needed) Script it out for them, give them guidelines, target questions to ask as an interviewer. One student is the interviewer and the other student gets interviewed. They can do this quietly at their seats or take turns to do at the front of the class. The next day in class, have the same activity, but have the students reverse roles. The interviewer is now getting interviewed and the interviewed is now the interviewer.

22. **Listen to some popular English music.** (Some popular English music) Write out the song lyrics for your class and discuss what they mean. Now, sing the song together as a class.

23. **Go to the school computer as a class and watch or do something English on it.** (A computer with the internet) There are a lot of great English websites. For learning, watching or whatever.

24. **Write a short speech on something you specify.** (No props needed) Then, each student needs to come to the front and read their speech to the class.

25. **Write a short story on anything they want.** (No props needed) You can edit it, they re-write it. Then, put the good copy of their story and hang them up on the classroom wall.

26. **Research a topic and do a presentation on your topic.** (No props needed) They can do research on their favorite singer, their favorite movie star, their favorite food, their family, their country etc. Encourage them to bring in props. Have each student do their presentation on a different day at school. So that each class is someone's day for their presentation. At the end of the presentation have the class ask questions and have a discussion for as long as you can.

27. **Make a class newspaper.** (Use big pieces of paper and fold into newspaper sized pages) Each student is responsible for their own section of the newspaper. Someone can do weather, someone else sports, local news, international news etc. When you are finished, you can put it on display at the front of your school.
28. **Walk to the local convenient store, buy some light candy and come back to class for an 'English only' class party.** (Some money, a convenient store) This can be a big reward for something good they did.

Activities For Younger Students (Under 10 years old)

1. **Play duck, duck, goose.** (No props needed) Have all the students sit in a circle facing inwards on the floor. Choose one student to stand up and walk around the circle touching each student on the head while saying "duck, duck, duck etc." When that student touches a student's head and says "goose". That student must stand up and they both start running around the circle. The first student to sit back down in the empty seat is safe. The student who was too slow to sit down must now be the one to go around the circle touching heads and saying "duck, duck, duck, duck, goose." This activity can go on and on as long as you want it to.

2. **Play Freeze.** (No props needed) Have all the kids stand up and move around the classroom shaking their body. Or you can tell them to pretend to be different animals & objects. You tell them to be a fish, a tiger, a cat, a dog, a snake, a table, a tree etc. Then, when the teacher shouts "freeze!" all the students must stop moving and talking. You can also use a whistle for this activity. Keep playing and telling your class what animal or object to be next. There is no winner or loser it is just something for your students to do. It's fun!

3. **Throw balls everywhere activity.** (A big box of balls) Just take a box of balls and stand up and dump the balls all over your classroom. Your students need to chase the balls everywhere and find them. They clean up all the balls and put them back in the box. The activity will then be over, unless you dump the box out again for a second time. You can also have them organize the balls into different groups of colors. Put all the red balls over here, put all the green balls over there etc.

4. **Stand up, show me your finger.** (No props needed) Have all your students stand up and have them show you their index finder. Tell them to go and touch something yellow, big, round, square, tall etc. Keep changing what you want them to find as they go all over your classroom trying to find it.

5. **Go for a walk, swim, and fly then see a scary animal and run away.** (No props needed) Stand up at the front of your class and tell all your students to stand up as well. Tell them they will go for a walk. Pretend like you are walking and talk about all the things you see along the way. "Look over there" as you point, "can everyone see the big yellow sun?" Then, you see a bear! "Ahhh" "Run, run, run" as you run as fast as you can on the same spot. Jump into the water and swim, swim, swim. Pretend you are swimming. Then you see a shark! "Ahhh" "Swim, swim, swim" as you swim as fast as you can on the same spot. Jump up and fly away. Fly back to the school. Go into your classroom, lie on the floor and go to sleep.

6. **Head / shoulders / knees and toes.** (No props needed) Stand up and sing this song with actions normally, then fast, then slow, then loud, then quiet, then pretend to be crying while you sing. You can also do this with other songs too.

7. **Read them a story.** (A story book) Choose one student to go to the book section of your school and choose any

storybook they want. Now, read it to the class. During the reading, let them get involved with discussion and telling you their ideas and what they see in the book, what they are thinking about. Make it an active listening and discussing event, not just a passive listening activity. Children love storybooks, so read to your class often. Choose another student to put back the first book, and choose another book. Keep reading on.

8. **Color a picture on the whiteboard for your students to see.** (No props needed) Use as many different colored markers that you can find. Draw a big picture on the whiteboard. Describe what you are drawing while you draw it. Ask your class questions, let them talk, get them involved, let them discuss it with you.

9. **Have a child come up to whiteboard and draw something for you.** (No props needed) Some of the students in your class will be good drawers. They like to come up to the front and draw for the class. So, at appropriate times during your class just ask "Does anyone know how to draw a (something)? Then, let that child come up and draw it instead of you.

10. **Puppets talking show.** (2 or 3 puppets) Hide behind the whiteboard or something solid and do a puppet show for your children to watch and listen to. Make it up as you go along.

11. **Count anything and everything possible.** (No props needed) Go for a walk around the school and just count things, count anything and everything. Count as a class, have the students count and tell you how many, or have just one student go and count something then report it to the class.

12. **Read anything and everything possible.** (No props needed) Go around the school reading the walls, reading other classrooms, read anything and everything you can.

13. **Review how to tell time on a clock.** (A real clock or a toy clock that you can move the big and small hand around). Make sure you explain it as plain and simple as you can at first. Then, build up to the more complex part of the clock later. This is a concept that takes a long time to catch on to. You can also have them all make clocks for an arts & crafts class, now the whole class can practice together on their own clocks.

14. **Draw or color in a picture.** (A picture to be colored and then photocopy one for each student in your class) When they are finished, the child can take it home or you can hang them on the wall.

15. **Make some sort of arts & craft.** (glue, tape, decorations, paper, sticks, yarn, etc.) The students can bring it up to the front of class when they are finished and explain what they have made. How did they make it? What materials did they use? Who will they give it to? Etc.

16. **Make paper airplanes and color them.** (Some paper, some crayons) Go out to the open area in your school and have paper airplane races. Who can throw their airplane the farthest?

17. **Play catch with a friend.** (A ball for each pair of students) Play in the most open area you can find in your school or outside. Teach them how to throw a ball and how to catch a ball. Then, pair the students up with each other and let them practice.

18. **Play with bubbles or balloons.** (Bring a few bottles of bubble to class). Go outside and blow bubbles for a while. Or bring some balloons to class. Blow them up and go to the open area in your school. Just hit the balloons around trying to keep them in the air, don't let them touch the ground.

19. **Stretching.** (A CD player, some children's music) Play background music from a CD. Stand up and stretch

while listening to music. Stretch your arms, legs, back etc.

20. **Jump this way 3 times, jump that way three times, sit down, stand up, etc.** (No props needed) Ask your students to follow your directions. Stand at the front of the class and ask them to do anything and everything you can possibly come up with. Example: go under the table, sit down, stand up, roll over, touch the wall, jump like a rabbit, jump this way 3 times, just forwards 4 time etc.

21. **Hoola Hoop Game.** (3 to 4 hoola hoops) The teacher stands behind a line and so does the child. The teacher spins out one hoola hoop at a time. When the hoola hoop comes back, the child has to catch it. Roll all 4 hoops and see how many the child can catch.

22. **Go for a jog.** (No props needed) If your class is getting hyper or has been sitting down too long, go for a jog. Take the class around your school in single file, or take them outside to an open and safe area. The safer the area, the faster they can run. The smaller the area, make sure they don't run fast and tell them to be extra careful.

23. **Kick ball around pylons and then into a net.** (Some pylons, some balls, a net) The teacher can be the goalie. Let your students go one at a time, maneuvering the ball around the pylons and then to kick the ball on net. Let them score often as it will make them feel good and build their confidence.

24. **Do some physical activities.** (No props needed) Play ball games or physically active games in the open area at your school or go outside. Example: play a simple version of baseball with a light bat and ball and only 2 bases, home plate and first base. Kick the ball where you have a child come up and just kick the ball. Play a simple game of soccer etc.

25. **Sing children songs from your CD's.** (A CD player, children songs) Sing many different songs and use actions

for each and every song you sing. The teacher leads at the front and all the children follow your actions as you sing. Or you can choose 1 or 2 well behaved students to come up and lead.

26. **Make an obstacle course.** (a bunch of obstacles to challenge your students) The students have to navigate their way through it. Start on this line, then go under the table, over this chair, take the spoon and put the ball in it. Carry the ball to this basket. Then, run backwards to the finish line and have the next student go. You can also time the children to see how many seconds it takes them to complete the course.

27. **Play house.** (A bunch of toys, walls, blankets, balls, books, CD player with children's music CD's etc.) When you really need to get a break from class. Go to an open area in your school and make a house or play area. Play some background music. Have some toy cars for the children to drive around in. Get some balls and throw them everywhere. Bring out some books, make a bridge with a blanket, use anything and everything you can think of. Then, just let the children play for 15 to 20 minutes. Remember to tell them to speak only English though.

28. **Have outings.** (No props needed) Go to the park, go for a walk, go to a different classroom, go upstairs, go downstairs, do anything to get your students up and doing things, it just makes things more fun.

Songs to Sing

Songs to Sing for Younger Children (Under 10 years old)

1. Teach these songs with actions. Get everyone to stand up and follow the teacher as you sing through the lyrics.
2. If you do not know one of these songs, look it up on the internet and find the lyrics. There will be even more songs online, and also a chance for you to hear the tune of each song or nursery rhyme you want to teach your class.

Example of Songs / Nursery Rhymes to Sing

1. Head, Shoulders, Knees & Toes
2. If You're Happy and You Know It Clap Your Hands
3. Row, Row, Row Your Boat: Gently Down the Stream
4. Twinkle Twinkle Little Star
5. I'm a Little Teapot
6. You Are My Sunshine
7. The Wheels on the Bus Go Round and Round
8. Skidamarink-E-Dink E-Dink, Skidamarink-E-Do
9. Ring Around the Rosie
10. Do the Hokey Pokey and Turn Yourself Around
11. B-I-N-G-O
12. Old MacDonald Had a Farm E I E I O
13. Eeny, Meeny, Miny, Moe: Catch a Tiger By the Toe
14. Hush, Little Baby Don't Say a Word
15. Itsy Bitsy Spider
16. There Was an Old Lady Who Swallowed a Fly

17. There's a Hole in my Bucket
18. Brush Your Teeth
19. Hickory Dickory Dock
20. Humpty Dumpty
21. Jack and Jill
22. London Bridge is Falling Down
23. Mary Had a Little Lamb
24. My Bonnie Lies over the Ocean
25. This Old Man, He Played One
26. One, Two, Buckle My Shoe

Wiggle, Wiggle Your Fingers

1. Wiggle, wiggle, wiggle your fingers as slowly as you can. Now wiggle your fingers as quickly as you can! Shake, shake, shake your hands as slowly as you can. Now shake your hands as quickly as you can! Jump, jump, jump... etc.

Walking Walking (Sang to the tune of Frere Jacques)

1. Walking, Walking. Walking, walking. Jump, jump, jump. Jump, jump, jump. Running, running, running. Running, running, running. Now let's stop, now let's stop.

Hello Teacher (Sang to the tune of Frere Jacques)

1. Hello Teacher, Hello Teacher. How are you? How are you? I am fine, thank you. I am fine, thank you. And you? And you?

Good-bye Teacher (Sang to the tune of Frere Jacques)
1. Good-bye Teacher. Good-bye Teacher. See you soon.
   See you soon. Good-bye Teacher. Good-bye Teacher.
   See you again. See you again.

Are you Sleeping Boys and Girls
(Sang to the tune of Frere Jacques)
1. Are you sleeping? Are you sleeping? Boys and girls. Boys
   and girls. Time to pay attention. Time to pay attention.
   Follow me. Follow me.

Telephone song (Example students: Kim and Peter)
Class: Hey Peter!

Peter: I think I hear my name

Class: Hey Peter!

Name: I think I hear it again

Class: You're wanted on the telephone. If you are busy, then who
is home?

Peter: (Says another classmate's name): Kim

(Now start the song over again substituting the name with Kim)